Glenn Wilson was born in
Graduating from Canterbu
M.A. with first class hono
professional theatre in Ne
singer. He then took up a
Institute of Psychiatry, U
PhD. in 1970. Since then h
at the Institute, and for a short time in ...
Director of the Psychology Clinic at the California State
University in Los Angeles.

Dr. Wilson has published some 70 articles on abnormal,
personality and social psychology as well as three books
on similar subjects.

ACKNOWLEDGEMENTS

The test items appearing in this book were initially designed for use in the ATV series 'I.Q. You'. I am grateful to ATV Network Limited for permission to reprint them here.

I am indebted to Hans Eysenck for his helpful interest and for the many fruitful discussions about the nature of intelligence held during preparations for our daily duels on the tennis court. Thanks also go to John Jones for trying out these problems on his adult education classes and to my many colleagues and ex-friends who acted as guinea-pigs during early pilot runs.

Glenn Wilson

Improve Your I.Q.

Futura Publications Limited

A Futura Book

First published in Great Britain in 1974
by Futura Publications Limited
Reprinted 1975, 1977, 1978
Copyright © Glenn Wilson 1974

This book is sold subject to the condition
that it shall not, by way of trade or
otherwise, be lent, re-sold, hired out or
otherwise circulated without the publisher's
prior consent in any form of binding or
cover other than that in which it is
published and without a similar condition
including this condition being imposed on the
subsequent purchaser.

ISBN 0 8600 7026 3
Printed in Great Britain by
Hazell Watson & Viney Ltd
Aylesbury, Bucks

DEDICATED TO DAVID NIAS

INTRODUCTION

In 1971 ATV in the Midlands ran a series of IQ-type quizzes which enjoyed a considerable amount of popularity. The series was called "IQ You", and the idea was that small groups representing various occupations would compete against each other in a trial of brain power. For example, a group of traffic wardens would take on some professional footballers to find out which occupational group would emerge as superior at solving a common set of problems. As a result of the success of this series it was decided to present the original set of 130 problems in book form so that they might be used for a variety of purposes ranging from parlour games and mental exercise to testing one's own IQ and sharpening one's ability to handle tests of this kind, if and when they should be encountered as selection devices in an occupational or educational setting. Because of the medium for which these puzzles were initially designed they have been geared to entertainment as well as brain-taxing; however, despite some apparent flippancy and the topicality of some of the material incorporated in them, these problems are sufficiently close to the items used in standard IQ tests to be good measures of intelligence and good practice for tackling other tests of intelligence.

The title of this book suggests that it will enable people to improve their performance on intelligence tests. How can this be if intelligence is largely a quality that we are born with and which remains fixed and immutable throughout life? The answer is that intelligence as an "ideal" scientific concept does remain fairly stable, but IQ tests, as most of us know them, are not pure measures of genetic potential. Within certain limits they are influenced by environmental factors. Among the most important of these influences are educational experience and practice on the kind of problems which are used in the tests. This book has been set up in such a way that

5

readers can demonstrate the latter effect to themselves. A scoring system has been given for two tests out of the thirteen, the first and the last, based on a time restriction of 10 minutes for each. The reader may like to toss a coin to decide whether he does Test 1 or Test 13 first; whichever one is tackled first, it should be followed by Tests 2 to 12 (in any order and without time restriction). Performance on the remaining test (either 1 or 13 depending on which has been done first) can then be used to gauge any improvement in IQ score resulting from the practice obtained between taking the two tests. This of course is provided the 10-minute limit is observed for each of the two comparison tests. It also needs to be stressed that the appropriate comparison is between the two IQ scores calculated from the conversion tables given in the back, not between the two "raw scores" obtained by counting up the number of correct answers. This is because the two tests differ slightly in overall difficulty, a correction for which is built into the conversion table.

Another caution necessary at the outset is that this comparison will not always provide evidence of an improvement in every individual case. It will certainly do so if we are comparing the average scores of a large enough group of people, and the chances are high that any individual (e.g. the present reader) will also find his second score higher than his first. However, occasional results in which performance on the first test appears superior will occur for two reasons: Firstly, there is an element of error or unreliability in all psychological testing. In the present case, for example, one might have a lucky break in getting a question that involves a knowledge of musical instruments when one happens to be a professional musician. Or, a highly intelligent person might go on a wrong tack looking for a complex solution to a problem because the right answer seemed banal or "obvious". These random errors are normally expected to cancel out over a number of test items, so the more items in the test the less error will affect the final score. By usual standards our two tests are fairly short, containing only ten items each and giving only 10-minute samples of intellectual effort. Therefore it is possible for enough error to accumulate to overthrow the expectation of a higher score on the second-done test. For a more reliable estimate of his IQ the reader is recommended to use the table based on the total scores obtained in Tests 1 and 13; this is based on 20 items and 20 minutes' work and is therefore considerably more stable. In fact, we can say with a high degree of confidence that the IQ score obtained by this method is unlikely to be more than 10 points removed from the "true" IQ of the subject.

A second reason why improvement may fail to appear from one test to the next is that the reader may already have had an asymptotic (saturation level) amount of experience with problems of this type. As we have said, there is a definite limit on the extent to which practice with IQ tests will result in an increase in score; once this has been reached no further improvement will occur and the IQ will stabilize. Readers who have taken several IQ tests in the past or who have spent a great deal of their leisure time pitting their wits against problems of this kind can expect less benefit in terms of elevated IQ scores as a result of working through this book. People who have not previously encountered a test of this kind, on the other hand might find their final score markedly improved. Under these conditions an increase of about 8 IQ points can be expected on average. When Professor H. J. Eysenck produced "Know Your Own IQ" which was the first properly standardized yet openly available intelligence test of this kind, he defended it partly on this ground. He felt that since IQ tests were being widely used for selection purposes in education and industry (where their usefulness is well established) it was unfair that some individuals should have the advantage of familiarity with them when others did not.

7

It was well known that some applicants obtained professional or "inside" help which prepared them for the kind of questions that they would be confronted with when called upon to take IQ tests, if not coaching on the actual tests themselves. The latter practice, which involves the unauthorized release of confidential test materials, is clearly outside of the ethical code of professional psychologists, but the relevant professional organizations in both the U.K. and U.S.A. have agreed that publication of IQ tests which allow rehearsal on items *similar* to those employed in standard, protected instruments is perfectly legitimate and possibly even desirable.

The 130 problems presented herein are arranged into 13 sets of 10 problems each, corresponding to the 13 programmes in the "IQ You" series. Because these 13 tests are of approximately equal difficulty they may be found particularly useful as party games and contests of one sort or another which require fairly equivalent sets of problems. Answers for all items are given in the back of the book. Ambiguity and the problem of alternative solutions have been minimized as far as possible by trying them out on groups of people known to differ *a priori* in their level of intelligence and assessing the various answers given by them. Nevertheless, it has to be conceded that ambiguity can never be completely eliminated in an intelligence test; someone is certain to come up with an alternative answer that seems equally or more correct, at least in their own opinion. Unfortunately, this has to be treated as another source of error and the official scoring system adhered to. It may seem unjust in certain specific cases, but unless the referee's decision is accepted (with or without good grace) the game simply cannot be played at all.

For people interested in estimating their own IQ this can be done by taking Tests 1 and 13, allowing themselves a time limit of only 10 minutes on each, and converting the total number of correct answers from the two tests combined into an IQ score by referring to the conversion table given in the back of the book (Table 1). This IQ score is only an estimate; being based on a limited sample of intellectual performance it will be accurate only within a certain range (perhaps 10 points in either direction). Readers who wish to check this score are referred to Eysenck's two Pelican's "Know Your Own IQ" and "Check Your Own IQ" which provide a similar set of problems with instructions for self-scoring. If all three tests give a similar score then the reader can be fairly sure that this is reliable; if they give widely divergent figures then the best estimate of the "true" IQ would be an average of them, but more un-certainty would have to be allowed. A discussion of the meaning of IQ scores is given in the last section of the book. For people who wish to work through these prob-lems simply for personal satisfaction or mental exercise the time limits attached to tests 1 and 13 are not relevant, but the answers given by the author as correct may still be of some interest.

Finally, a word about the difficulty of these problems. As you will probably soon discover, they are by no means easy. Even people who fancy themselves as ex-ceptionally high in intelligence are likely to have trouble answering more than about half of the items in each test in reasonable time, and some items will be beyond their power in the sense that even protracted effort will not be rewarded. A great variety of different strategies and thinking processes are demanded by these tests — some of them far from orthodox. This warning is given at the outset in the hope that the realistic anticipation of dif-ficulty will reduce the incidence of nervous breakdown resulting from acute demoralization and frustration in the pages that follow.

SUMMARY OF INSTRUCTIONS
FOR SELF-SCORING THE IQ

1. Tests 1 and 13 are the critical ones. Do not dip into them if you are interested in testing your IQ.
2. Take these two tests in a quiet setting allowing a strict time limit of 10 minutes for each.
3. Score them by referring to the answers in the back of the book.
4. Add the scores obtained in tests 1 and 13 and convert to IQ using Table 1.
5. *For assessing improvement due to practice,* toss a coin. If it comes up heads start with Test 1 (again allowing a strict 10 minutes), score and convert to IQ using Table 2; then do Tests 2 to 12 in your own time, and finish with Test 13 — also timed at 10 mins, and converted to IQ using Table 3. If the coin comes up tails, the same procedure is followed except that Test 13 is done first and Test 1 follows practice on the intervening eleven tests.

TEST 1

Which is the odd one out?

PHI

PSI

PI

CHI

SHI

XI

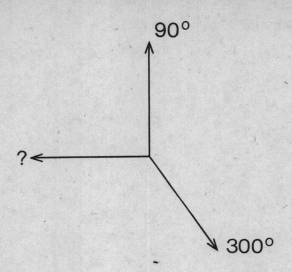

Find the missing letter.

EARTH	CAN
MEAT	DEAF
CAN	EASE
LEFT	QUAKE
STRIP	AXE
TONE	HAND

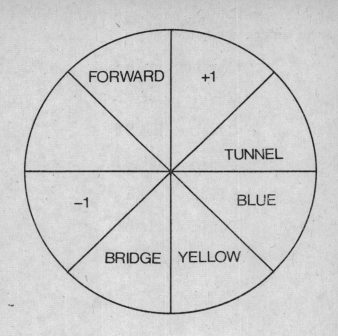

What is the missing letter?

THEBE TERP ART

OFVAL OUR ISD

IS CRET ION

What is the next number in the series?

0, .5, .87, 1, .87, .5, 0, -.5,

Complete the following;

A_1w	B_2x	C_3y	D_4z
B_4y	A_3z	D_2w	C_1x
C_2z	D_1y	A_4x	B_3w
D_3x	C_4w	B_1z	

Which is the odd one out?

JO	NG
JACK	DEAN
ALBERT	OGBORN
MARK	WEIL
SYLVESTER	WAKEFIELD
SAM	YEE
VALENTIN	GOLDBERG
VICTOR	ORTEGA
MAX	WILKINSON
RAY	LEE
HAROLD	MALLOY
MAURICE	FRIEDEN

What is the missing number?

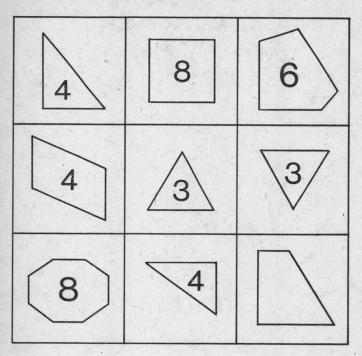

What is the missing word?

TASK (FAG) CIGARETTE

TOW (　　　) TRANSVESTITISM

TEST 2

Which is the odd one out?

TUATARA

PTARMIGAN

PTERODACTYL

PLATYPUS

MOA

MARSUPIAL

HIPPOPOTAMUS

MOUSE

Find a two-letter word that completes the first word and starts the second.

ORB (   ) SELF

What is the next number in the series?

1, 2, 5, 26, ?

Which is the odd one out?

EARTH

MOON

MARS

SATURN

ASTEROID

JUPITER

CONSTANTINOPLE is to ISTANBUL
as ST PETERSBURG is to . . .

What is the missing number?

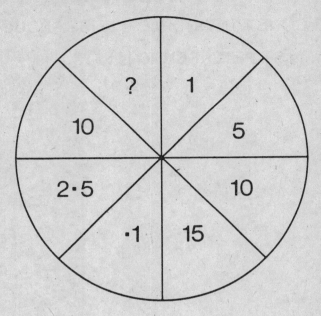

Which is the odd one out?

A

B

C

D

E

F

G

H

A normal coin is tossed 9 times in succession and comes down tails each time. What are the chances that it will come down heads the next time?

What is the missing number?

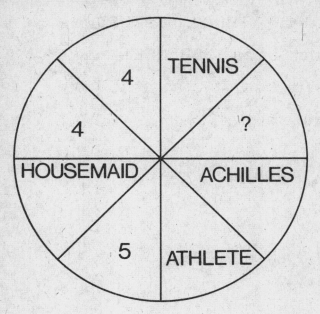

THRILL is to THRILLER

as SUSPENSE is to . . .

TEST 3

Which is the odd one out?

SEMPRE

FORTE

VIVACE

CHIANTI

ALLEGRO

MOLTO

MOSSO

What four-letter word inserted in the brackets completes
the first word and begins the second?

HARM (   ) ON

Find the next two letters in the series:

A, C, F, J, ?, ?

What is the missing number?

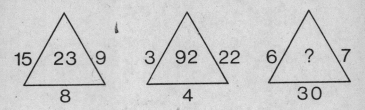

Which is the odd one out?

INSUBORDINATE

DEPOPULATION

PNEUMONIA

DENUNCIATORY

FUNCTIONATE

TETRADACTYLOUS

TESTUDINARIOUS

EFFICACIOUS

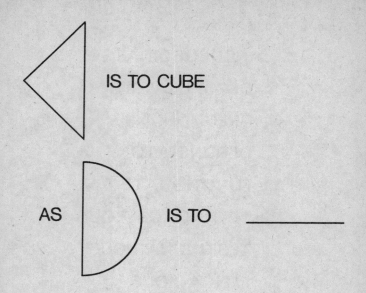

IS TO CUBE

AS IS TO _____

Find the next two letters in the series

A, K, Q, J, T, ?, ?

Find the missing word.

1	2	3	4	5	6	7	1	5	8	9
T	R	E	P	I	D	A	T	I	O	N

4	10	5	11	8	12	8	4	10	3	2
P	H	I	L	O	S	O	P	H	E	R

5	9	6	13	12	1	2	5	8	13	12

What is the missing letter?

HDRALD   WELTO

EAWORD   HIASH?

QUAD is to OCT

as TRI is to . . .

TEST 4

Which is the odd one out?

IMBECILE

IDIOT

CRETIN

NINCOMPOOP

GENIUS

FOOL

INTELLECTUAL

What three-letter word completes the first word and begins the second?

CAP (   ) RENT

What is the missing number?

9	2	6	8	7	8
7	6	7	5	1	?

Which is the odd one out?

TREE

BIRD

ROCK

MUSHROOM

WORM

WOMAN

MY FAIR LADY is to SHAW

as WEST SIDE STORY is to . . . .

What is the missing number?

Which is the odd one out?

PURPLE

RED

ORANGE

GREEN

YELLOW

BLUE

Complete the following:

$$1 + 5 + 8 = N$$

$$3 - 2 + 11 = L$$

$$7 + 11 - 5 = M$$

$$20 - 6 + 2 =$$

EINS	10	VITY
BELL	5	HONE
MARC	4	ADIO
CURI	?	DIUM

CRACK is to CRACKERS

as NICK is to ...

TEST 5

Which is the odd one out?

BORON

NEON

LITHIUM

EINSTEINIUM

HELIX

ARSENIC

SULPHUR

LEAD

OXYGEN

Find a two-letter word which completes the first word and starts the second.

QUIET (   ) HER

What is the next item in the series?

2.4,   5.3,   8.2,   11.1,   ?

Supply the missing word.

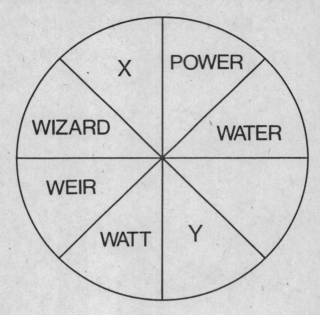

LILLIPUTIAN is to GARGANTUAN
as HYPO is to ...

What is the missing word?

BOG+2−0= DOG

FAG+1−5= GAB

BIG +4−0= FIG

GOD+0−2= ?

Which is the odd one out?

SHOW BOAT

CAROUSEL

MY FAIR LADY

PAINT YOUR WAGON

SOUND OF MUSIC

OLIVER

KISS ME KATE

SOUTH PACIFIC

How many triangles are there in the figure below?

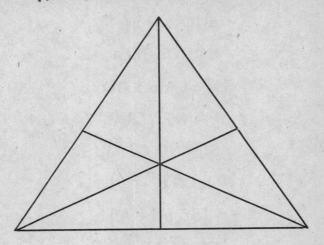

CHOLERIC is to BILE

as SANGUINE is to ...

If Mary Tynan married Kenneth Whitehouse who would marry Vanessa Muggeridge?

TEST 6

Which is the odd one out?

BRITAIN

FRANCE

WEST GERMANY

NETHERLANDS

BELGIUM

LUXEMBOURG

ITALY

EIRE

Find a three-letter word which completes the first word and begins the second.

FIRE (   ) CHAIR

What is the next item in the series?

$$-6, \ 2, \ -\frac{2}{3}, \ \frac{2}{9}, \ (?)$$

What is the missing word?

TREE (LIFE) ORANGUTANG

BOTANY (BIOLOGY) ECOLOGY

POPINJAY (   ) PARROT

COPRA is to COCO

as COCOA is to ...

What number should go in position x?

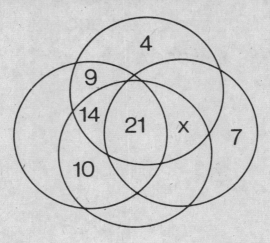

Which is the odd one out?

BRASS

BRONZE

STEEL

IRON

AMALGAM

How many squares are there in the diagram below?

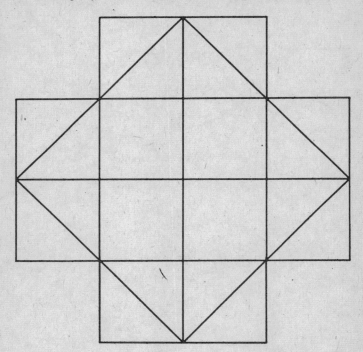

What is the missing word?

PEARE DIVER (MACBETH) SHAKES

THE GOODUN (   ) GOE

GOOD is to NAUGHTY

as PIANO is to . . .

Which is the odd one out?

RIVER

RAINBOW

CLOUD

WATERFALL

MOAT

MOUNTAIN

FOREST

What is the missing word?

FOUR (TEEN) AGE

DOWN (   ) LORD

What is the missing number?

2	13	5	11
−1		5	

HALF is to TRIPLE

as THIRD is to (   )

What is the missing word?

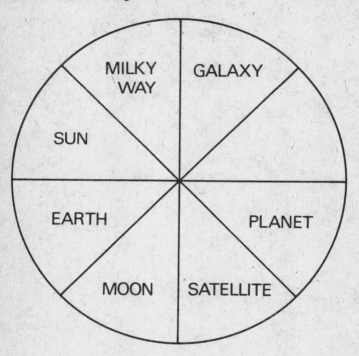

What is the next number in the series?

$$2, \; 1\tfrac{1}{3}, \; \tfrac{2}{3}, \; 0, \; (?)$$

A man is born when his father is 27 years old. How old will he be when he is exactly half his father's age?

Which is the odd one out?

TURQUOISE

DIAMOND

RUBY

EMERALD

GOLD

SILVER

BRONZE

What is the missing letter?

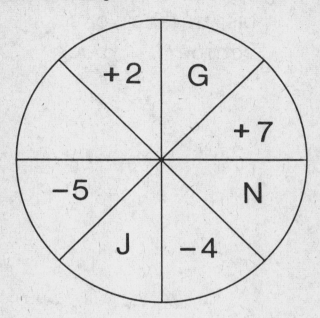

What is the missing word?

DISMISS (SACK) BAG

DOCTOR (   ) DUCK

TEST 8

Which is the odd one out?

EREWHON

EREBUS

EMPYREUS

ELYSIUM

EL DORADO

HADES

LIMBO

LILLIPUT

SHANGRI LA

TIMBUCTU

CAMELOT

ATLANTIS

BRUTOPIA

What is the next number in the series?

6.75,   4.5,   3,   ?

What is the missing word?

EXHIBIT (OR) DEAL
MAD (　　) ASS

What word would complete the diagram below?

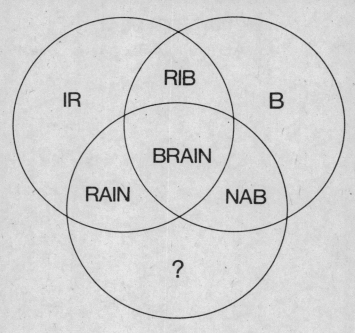

PHOTOPHOBIC is to DARKNESS
as HELIOTROPIC is to ...

Find the missing word. (Clue: AS QUICKLY AS POSSIBLE)

I	N	V	E	S	T	I	G	A	T	I	O	N
1	2	3	4	5	6	1	7	8	6	1	9	2
1	2	5	6	8	2	6	8	2	4	9	10	5

What is the missing letter?

```
        L    '    E         S    E    R
   L                   N                    V
E                      O                       A
W                      ?                       T
    O    P    H         E    V    I
```

Which is the odd one out?

ANAEMIA

ANOXIA

DIPSOMANIA

DIPHTHERIA

MALARIA

CINERARIA

CHOLERA

CLAUSTROPHOBIA

SCHIZOPHRENIA

GONORRHOEA

How many diamond shapes are there in the figure below?

Complete the limerick:

'TWAS ON THE GOOD SHIP VENUS

BY JOVE YOU SHOULD HAVE SEEN US

WE WERE FIFTY TWO

ON THE OCEAN BLUE

NOT A SINGLE GIRL . . .

TEST 9

Which is the odd one out?

ORAL

AURAL

NASAL

VISUAL

PEDAL

MANUAL

CRANIAL

BANAL

GENITAL

What is the next number in the series:

1,   4,   9,   61,   52,   ?

What is the missing word?

PARSON (AGE) LESS

SUN (   ) LIGHT

Complete the following:

What is the missing letter?

NEWS	TOP
HUM	PAPER
KEY	PET
BUS	BUG
CAR	HOLE

Find the missing number?

$$1 \quad 3 \quad 3 \quad 2$$

$$0 \quad 1 \quad 4 \quad 3$$

$$3 \quad 1 \quad 1 \quad 0$$

$$2 \quad 0 \quad 1 \quad ?$$

$$6 \quad 5 \quad 9 \quad 6$$

Which is the odd one out?

DAVID

WILLIAM

CHARLES

GEORGE

HENRY

ELIZABETH

ANNE

RICHARD

EDWARD

What is the missing number?

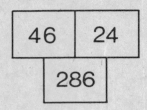

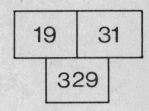

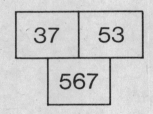

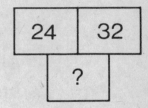

What number goes at the bottom point of the star?

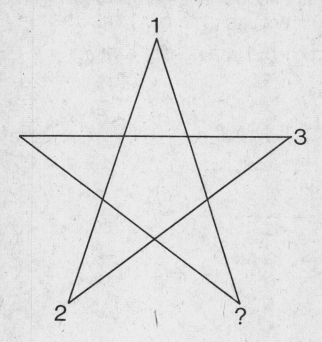

What is the missing word?

WALKS (STRIDES) TROUSERS

FEATHER ( ) GIRL

TEST 10

DAVID COPPERFIELD

OLIVER TWIST

NICHOLAS NICKLEBY

CHARLES DICKENS

SILAS MARNER

JAMES BOND

PETER GRIMES

ALBERT HERRING

JOHN FALSTAFF

What is the next number in the series?

15, 52, 26, 63, 37, ?

What is the missing word?

DON (KEY) STONE

HONEY (   ) STRUCK

What is the missing number?

Which is the odd one out?

LIQUID

OPAQUE

SOLID

QUIET

LOQUACIOUS

REQUEST

SERIOUS

HAPPY

What is the missing number?

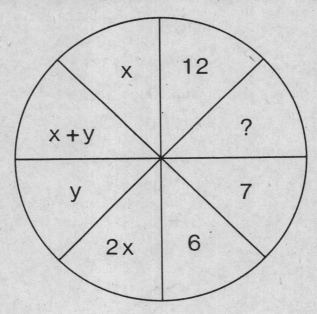

What is the missing letter?

HAM	ERG
HUM	RIFF
HAP	LET
MAN	LESS
ICE	OUR
MID	KIND

What is the missing number?

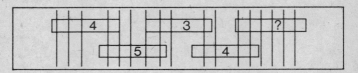

Which is the odd one out?

HASHISH

HEROIN

LSD

COCAINE

CAFFEINE

OPIUM

HELIUM

ALCOHOL

What is the missing word?

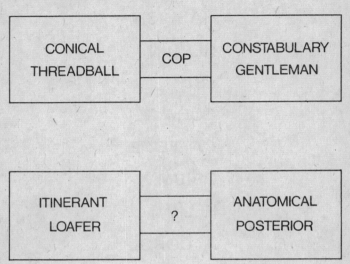

| CONICAL THREADBALL | COP | CONSTABULARY GENTLEMAN |

| ITINERANT LOAFER | ? | ANATOMICAL POSTERIOR |

TEST 11

Which is the odd one out?

AEROPLANE

CAT

CAMEL

CAR

SHIP

HORSE

COACH

What is the next number in the series?

10, 12, 32, 34, 54, 56, ?

What is the missing letter?

FOR	CAT
WORK	TICK
MAY	TUNE
PUSSY	RIGHT
YARD	SHOP
FORTH	POLE

What is the missing number?

	3		6		?		2	
4		15		17		13		7
	1		5		4		5	

Which is the odd one out?

TROCHEE

IAMB

DACTYL

SPECTRE

SPONDEE

How many different triangles are there in the figure below?

**SPHERE is to OVAL
as CUBE is to ...**

What word completes the diagram below?

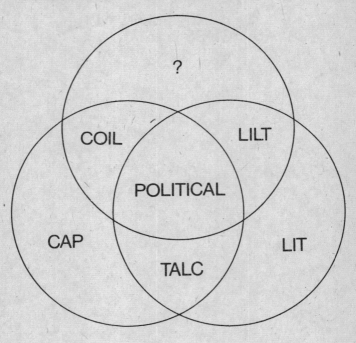

Which is the odd one out?

SPEECH

TELEPHONIST

TELEVISION

NEWSPAPER

POSTMAN

RADIO

REFRIGERATOR

What is the missing word?

SNOW (SLUSH) SENTIMENT

GARMENT (   ) ASSAULT

TEST 12

Which is the odd one out?

CENTURY

SECOND

MONTH

MINUTE

WEEK

YEAR

DECADENT

HOUR

DAY

What is the missing number?

1	3	6	12	24	30
$\frac{1}{2}$	1	$2\frac{1}{2}$	?	10	$12\frac{1}{2}$

Find the missing letter.

OURFA

THERW

HICHA

RTINH

EAVE

What is the missing number?

6	5	8	7	4
	15	20	28	?

Which is the odd one out?

SAMOA

FIJI

HAWAII

TAHITI

BERMUDA

JAPAN

NEW ZEALAND

NEW GUINEA

What is the missing number?

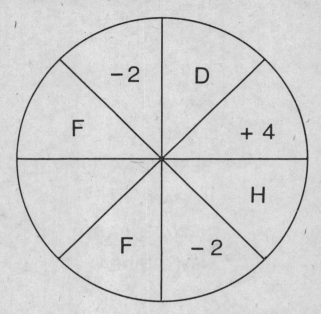

What is the missing word?

TORCH	FLASH	LIGHT
CAR	AUTO	MOBILE
LIFT	ELEVA	TOR
FOOT	PATH	SIDE

What are the missing letters?

CD	BF	AH
DF	CH	BJ
EH	DJ	?

Which is the odd one out?

HALF

ZERO

QUARTER

EQUAL

TRIPLE

SIXTEENTH

DOUBLE

What is the missing word?

CONTAINED (IN) FASHIONABLE

WHIP (FLOG) SELL

BEETLE (   ) PESTER

TEST 13

Which is the odd one out?

THROUGH

THOUGHT

THOROUGH

TROUGH

TOUGH

BOUGH

BROUGHT

Find a four-letter word (not indecent) that completes the first word and starts the second.

FORTH (   ) OUT

Find the missing number.

17	35	3	21
26		19		?

Which is the odd one out?

DALI

DA VINCI

VAN GOGH

VERDI

PICASSO

WALT DISNEY

AL CAPP

$2\frac{1}{2}$ is to QUINTUPLE

as 2 is to . . .

What is the missing number?

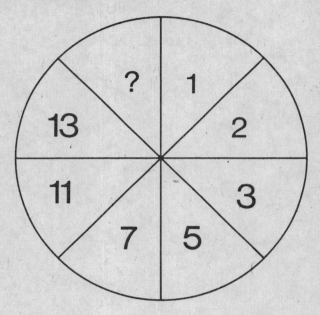

Which is the odd one out?

$$684 \cdot 5$$

$$\sqrt{100}$$

$$13 \cdot 4$$

$$-1$$

$$\sqrt{-49}$$

$$72$$

Which of the four clocks in the bottom line completes
the series in the top line?

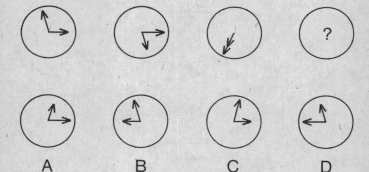

A   B   C   D

What is the missing number?

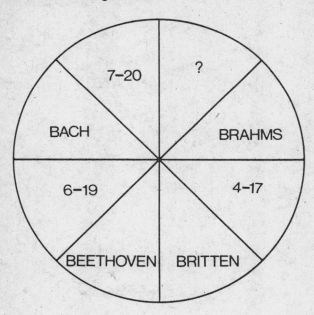

INFANT is to INFANCY

as ADULT is to ...

ANSWERS AND EXPLANATIONS:
TESTS 1—13

Test 1

SHI is not a Greek letter.

180° (Assume total of 360°, then direction must be anti-clockwise).

T (STRIP(T)EASE).

BACKWARD (Pattern of opposite relations).

T (The bet(t)er part of valour is discretion: *Henry IV, Part I*).

−.87 (30° values on sine curve).

A_2y (No item appears more than once in any row or column).

MAX WILKINSON (Others have equal number of letters in first name and surname).

6 (Number of sides on the figure plus the number of right angles).

DRAG (Words outside brackets fairly synonymous if only colloquially).

Test 2

MARSUPIAL is a *class* of animals, others are individual species (both PTERODACTYL and MOA are extinct; PTERODACTYL and PTARMIGAN both fly; MOUSE and HIPPO are both mammals. Therefore these answers are not correct).

IT (Orbit, itself).

677 (Each number generated by squaring the previous number and adding one).

MOON is an Earth satellite, others are in solar orbit.

LENINGRAD

22.5 (The numbers in the left half are obtained by squaring the opposite number and dividing by 10).

G (Others are all symmetrical across a horizontal dividing line).

50% or .5 (The probability on a given occasion is not dependent on previous outcomes).

4 (Tennis-elbow: 5 letters; Achilles-heel: 4 letters; Athlete-foot: 4 letters; Housemaid-knee: 4 letters).

SUSPENDER (The comical answer is accepted because there is no other more correct alternative).

Test 3

CHIANTI is a wine or a district, the others are Italian words which appear regularly as musical directions.

LESS (Harmless, lesson).

O, U (There is one letter in the alphabet between A and C, two letters between C and F, and so on).

34 (Add the numbers outside the triangle and write backwards).

TETRADACTYLOUS (All the others contain all five vowels).

SPHERE (Add the mirror image of the two-dimensional figure and raise it to the third dimension).

N, E. (Ace, king, queen, etc.).

INDUSTRIOUS (Simple letter-number coding using the first two words as keys. The one extra letter added in the third word, coded 13, is U, which can be interpolated on inspection of the rest of the word decoded).

N (The two lines are HAROLD WILSON and EDWARD HEATH with alternate letters exchanged so that they interlock. The N on the end of Wilson is missing).

SEX or HEX (Latin roots for 4, 8, 3, and 6 respectively).

Test 4

CRETIN   is biologically specific; others are behavioural evaluations.

TOR   (Captor, torrent: A tor is a rocky peak).

8 (The second row is obtained by subtracting 1 from each digit in the first row and listing in reverse order).

ROCK   is non-living object.

SHAKESPEARE   (Based on *Romeo and Juliet*).

3 (Count the number of "points" on each figure).

PURPLE   is *extra-spectral*, i.e. cannot be obtained by a single wave-length, only by mixing the two ends of the spectrum.

P   (L = 12th letter in alphabet: M = 13, N = 14, O = 15, P = 16).

3 (EINS/TEIN RELATI/VITY, 10 letters missing from the middle. BELL/TELEP/HONE, 5 letters, MARC/ONI R/ADIO, 4 letters, CURI/E RA/DIUM, 3 letters).

(K)NICKERS (Although the fear of looking silly may have caused hesitation, there is no more logical alternative).

Test 5

HELIX   is a spiral, the others are all elements.
US   (Quietus, usher).
14   (Add 2.9 to the preceding item).
WITCH   (The entries in the four upper sectors have an associated concept in the opposite sectors that sound similar to the query terms: Where, Why, What, Which).
HYPER   (Relationship is that of simple opposites).
GOB   (The plus sign raises the first letter of the word through the alphabet by the appropriate number, while the minus sign takes the last letter of the word back through the alphabet by the appropriate number. The middle letter does not change).
16

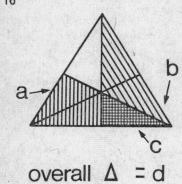

a x 6
b x 6
c x 3
d x 1
———
16

overall △ = d

BLOOD   (From Galen's description of personality based on the four "humours").
Malcolm Redgrave

Test 6

LUXEMBOURG   (Totally surrounded by land).
ARM   (Firearm, armchair).

$-\frac{2}{27}$ (multiply each item by $-\frac{1}{3}$

BIRD (The word in brackets is the concept which accommodates both the words outside at the lowest level of generalization).
CACAO (Copra and cacao are the products extracted from the Coco and Cacao trees respectively).
16

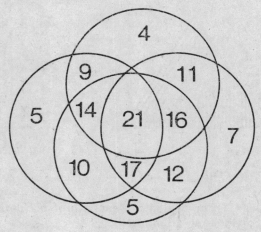

IRON is a pure (elemental) metal, others are alloys or mixtures of two or more basic metals.

18

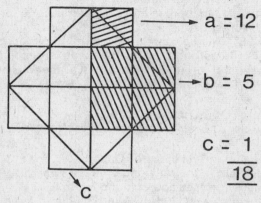

$$a = 12$$

$$b = 5$$

$$c = 1$$
$$\overline{18}$$

FAUST (The last and first words form SHAKES-PEARE and GOETHE. The second words are anagrams of the composers of operatic versions: VERDI and GOUNOD).

FORTE (Relation of opposites).

Test 7

MOAT   is manmade, the others are natural phenomena.

LAND   (Downland, landlord).

1   (Add the numbers in the two squares above and subtract the other two).

DOUBLE   (Multiply by 6).

STAR   (Items on left side are "home" examples of the more general terms on the right, e.g. the Milky Way is our own galaxy, etc.).

$-\frac{2}{3}$ (Subtract $\frac{2}{3}$ each time.)

27   (His father will then be 54).

DIAMOND   is the only one of these minerals which is not frequently used as a colour description.

E   (Going clockwise, N is 7 letters later in the alphabet after G, J is 4 letters before N, etc.).

QUACK   (Term in brackets is associated with both the words outside).

Test 8

TIMBUCTU (Has a present known existence—in the Sahara Desert, the others are mythical, fictional, or "lost").

2 (Multiply by 2/3, i.e. subtract half the previous item).

AM (Madam, amass).

AN (Where circles overlap the letters are combined so as to form meaningful words).

SUN or SUNLIGHT (Photophobia is aversion to light, heliotropism is movement towards the sun).

INSTANTANEOUS (Simple letter-number coding).

C (The two circles read ENOCH POWELL, and CONSERVATIVE).

CINERARIA is a flower, the others are diseases.

10 (Diamonds in this case are all squares).

BETWEEN US (No need to be vulgar).

Test 9

BANAL means commonplace, the others refer to some part of the body.

63 (Digits squared and written in reverse order).

DAY (Sun, daylight).

THE WILLOWS (Perceptual abbreviation may lead to the omission of THE).

S (The words pair off thus: newspaper, humbug, keyhole, carpet, bus(s)top).

1 (The first four digits in each column add to give the bottom digit).

DAVID (The others are names of English monarchs).

344 (Add together the two outside digits to give the middle digit below. Reverse the order of the other two digits to give the first and last digits respectively in the number below).

5 (The digits are in serial order linked from one to the next by a straight line. Thus 4 will be at the end of the straight line from 3, etc.).

BIRD (The word in brackets is a "common" associate of the words outside).

Test 10

CHARLES DICKENS is the name of an author, the others are fictional characters.

74 (The second digit of each pair is the same as the first digit of the following pair. These then form the simple series: 1, 5, 2, 6, 3, 7, etc.).

MOON (Honeymoon, moonstruck).

REQUEST is a verb, the others are states (adjectives).

1 (Relationship of opposite sectors is that of equality, thus:

$$2x = 12$$
$$x = 6$$
$$x+y = 7$$
$$\therefore \quad y = 1).$$

B (Hamlet, humour, hapless, mankind, ice(b)erg, midriff).

6 (The numbers in each rectangle correspond to the number of vertical lines passing through that rectangle).

HELIUM is an inert gas, the others are drugs which affect consciousness.

BUM

CAT (The others have all been used as means of transport).

76 (Add 2 and 20 alternately).

S (Fortune, workshop, maypole, pussycat, yard(s)tick, forthright).

2 (Numbers in middle row of bricks obtained by adding numbers from bricks touching above and below).

SPECTRE is a ghost, the others are metrical "feet" in poetry.

10

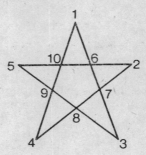

where no. is at apex of Δ

RECTANGLE (Reduce to two-dimensional form then elongate in one plane).

OIL (Words are formed by using letters obtained from overlapping circles).

REFRIGERATOR (The others are all concerned with communication).

SOCK (Words outside brackets are common associates of word inside; the latter more colloquial).

Test 12

DECADENT   is a condition, the others are periods of time.

5   (Decimal conversions of old penny values).

N   (Our father which art in heaven).

14   (Numbers below are half the product of the two above).

BERMUDA   is an Atlantic island; the others Pacific.

0   (Going clockwise each letter is forward or backward in the alphabet according to the number preceding it).

WALK   (English word followed by American equivalent).

CL   (First letter increase 1 going down; second letter increase 2 going down).

ZERO   is an absolute quantity; the others are relative.

BUG   (Words outside brackets are fairly synonymous, if only colloquially).

Test 13

THOROUGH   because it has two syllables (or two "O"s) or BOUGH because it does not contain the letter "t".

WITH   (Forthwith, without).

12   (Numbers in the lower squares are obtained by halving the total of the two above).

VERDI   is a composer, the others are best known in the visual arts.

QUADRUPLE

17   (The series consists of *prime numbers*, i.e. numbers which cannot be divided by any number other than themselves and one).

$\sqrt{-49}$ is an imaginary number; the others are real numbers. (The square root of any minus number is obscure in meaning because all numbers are positive when squared).

B   (Add on 2.20 each time).

9-18   (The first digit represents the number of letters in the composer's name. The second and third digits represent his century of birth).

ADULTHOOD   (Not adultery!).

Or MATURITY.

Table 1

For converting raw scores on Test 1 plus Test 13 into IQs

Score (*Total number correct*)	*IQ*
0	80—
1	84
2	88
3	93
4	98
5	102
6	107
7	112
8	117
9	121
10	126
11	131
12	135
13	140
14	145
15	150
16	155
17+	160+

Note: This table gives an estimate of IQ that applies reasonably well for English-speaking males and females aged 16 to 60; for people falling outside these criteria it may grossly underestimate the IQ.

Table 2

For converting raw scores on Test 1 into IQs

Score (Number correct)	IQ
0	82—
1	89
2	97
3	105
4	113
5	122
6	130
7	138
8	148
9+	155+

(see note on Table 1)

Table 3

For converting raw scores on Test 13 into IQs

Score (Number correct)	IQ
0	87
1	95
2	103
3	112
4	120
5	129
6	137
7	148
8+	155+

(see note on Table 1)

THE MEANING OF THE IQ: SOME FAVOURITE QUESTIONS ANSWERED

Intelligence ranks among the most explosively contro-
versial topics of our age. Only last year, Professor H. J.
Eysenck was about to commence a lecture on intelligence
at the London School of Economics when he was as-
saulted by a group of about 26 people who kicked him,
punched him, spat on him and broke his spectacles
before others were able to drag him clear. Researchers
in the U.S. who have espoused genetic theories of
intelligence (e.g. Jensen and Shockley) have been
subject to similar abuse. Apart from the heliocentric
theory of Copernicus and the Darwinian theory of
evolution, it is difficult to think of an area of scientific
enquiry that has aroused so much public excitement.
The reason seems to be that the field is seen to have far-
reaching political and social implications; just as earlier
developments in astronomy and biology appeared to
devalue mankind and threaten established religion,
recent evidence concerning the origins of intelligence is
viewed by many as likely to upset the prevailing political
philosophy. Historically it seems to be the case that
laymen offer violence towards scientists when they come
up with ideas that are both discomforting and well sup-
ported by the facts. A scientist who presents an un-
popular view that is not well substantiated can be
verbally rebuffed or simply dismissed as a crank; if he is
apparently talking the truth then a fist in the mouth may
be held necessary to silence him.

Whatever the reason may be, the current resurgence
of excitement about intelligence and its measurement
has not been accompanied by any appreciable degree of
enlightenment on the topic. Judging by the articles and
correspondence appearing in national newspapers and
journals, the time-worn myths remain, seeming to become progressively further entrenched with each re-

statement. What follows is concerned only with the factual evidence, or at least the best which is available to date, regardless of what social implications may be read into it. This is done not so much in a spirit of amorality as in the genuine belief shared by many scientists (and possibly held as their religion) that we should know the truth and "the truth will make us free". It is too much to hope that the following few pages will lay all popular fallacies to rest, but it is a sincere attempt to answer some of the most persistently recurring questions about the IQ clearly, concisely and dispassionately, with as much confidence as the current evidence permits.

What does the IQ tell us?

IQ stands for intelligence quotient. It is a score that gives an indication of how "bright" a person is compared to everyone else. The average IQ is by definition 100; scores above 100 indicate a higher than average IQ and scores below 100 indicate a lower than normal IQ. Theoretically, scores can deviate any amount below or above 100, but in practice, distinctions among scores below 50 and among scores above 150 are not very meaningful. These points then can be taken as the approximate limits on the distribution of IQ scores. The majority of people of course are grouped much closer to the 100 mark; in fact half of the population have IQs of between 90 and 110. Actually, the distribution of IQ scores follows approximately the bell-shaped curve that is typical of any variation for which the underlying causes are many and complex. This is called a "normal" curve (Fig. 1).

If IQs don't meaningfully go much above 150, how is it that some people boast extraordinarily high scores like 180 or 200? Unless they are established liars, the most likely explanation is that they were tested as children using a method for calculating the IQ that is now obsolete. When the French psychologist Alfred Binet was commissioned to construct the first IQ test for school-age children he observed that as children grow older their powers of problem solving tend to increase. Therefore he introduced the concept of "mental age". A child with a mental age of say 10 was one who could match the performance of the average ten-year-old on Binet's tests, whatever his actual (chronological) age might be. The first IQ scores were calculated as a ratio of mental age to chronological age (multiplied by 100 to remove the decimal point). For example, a 10-year-old child with a mental age of 13 would have an IQ of 130, while a 10-year-old child with a mental age of 7 would have an IQ of 70. This method of calculating the IQ can result in some exceedingly high (or low) figures, particularly when the denominator (age in years) is very low. For example, a one-year-old baby who can do what the normal two-year-old does comes out with an IQ of 200; this figure may then be quoted by his parents and subsequently himself, well into his adult years when it has ceased to have very much meaning. One of the main reasons for dropping the ratio method of calculating IQs is that it breaks down completely in adulthood, when the mental age stays level and even eventually declines, while chronological age moves on remorselessly. Modern IQ tests therefore use a statistical method for calculating IQs, based on the extent to which an indi-

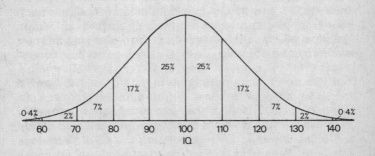

160

vidual's deviation from the average is itself atypical (i.e. its rareness). For example, an IQ of 140 is bettered by less than one person in 200. This can be seen in the figure above, where the numbers in the segments under the curve represent the percentage of the population included in that IQ range.

The concept of intelligence stems from the discovery that mental abilities of nearly all kinds are positively linked in the sense that if you are good at one thing you are also likely to be good at others. Thus if a person has a good memory there is a better than even chance that he has a good vocabulary, and that he is good at arithmetic. Similarly, if a person is good at arithmetic he probably also has a good memory and vocabulary. These associations do not always hold good, but they do on *average*, and this is what is meant by saying that all abilities are intercorrelated. IQ tests usually try to estimate this general ability by sampling performance on different kinds of cognitive skills (verbal, numerical, spatial, perceptual, etc.) and taking an overall average. (The total score works quite well as an average for this purpose provided the items evenly represent different types of ability.) Some ability tests actually give separate scores for a variety of specific abilities such as general knowledge, vocabulary, verbal reasoning, verbal fluency, numerical ability, spatial reasoning, mechanical ability, perceptual speed, memory, etc. This procedure is of theoretical interest and has some practical application in areas such as vocational guidance and the diagnosis of brain damage and specific disabilities. Nevertheless, different abilities are so closely linked that an overall measure of general intelligence is of much broader predictive value. For example, it is a very good indicator of how well a person will do on a course of higher education. A minimum IQ of 120 is probably necessary for a university first degree, and it would be extremely difficult to obtain a higher degree such as a doctorate with an IQ of less than 130. The only other predictor of academic success that comes at all close to IQ tests in terms of validity and usefulness is the individual's previous academic record. The connection here is obvious, but the major limitation of this approach is its lack of standardization; it is not easy to compare marks, grades and references given by different instructors and different institutions. IQ scores, on the other hand, are directly comparable no matter which school you come from.

A knowledge of IQ also gives a good indication of what the status of a person's eventual occupation is likely to be, though of course not the specific occupation itself. The following is a list of occupations typical of various IQ levels:

140	Higher Professional; Top Civil Servants; Professors and Research Scientists.
130	Lower Professional; Physicians and Surgeons; Lawyers; Engineers (Civil and Mechanical).
120	School Teachers; Pharmacists; Accountants; Nurses; Stenographers; Managers.
110	Foremen; Clerks; Telephone Operators; Salesmen; Policemen; Electricians; Precision Fitters.
100+	Machine Operators; Shopkeepers; Butchers; Welders; Sheet Metal Workers.
100—	Warehousemen; Carpenters; Cooks and Bakers; Small Farmers; Truck and Van Drivers.
90	Labourers; Gardeners; Upholsterers; Farmhands; Miners; Factory Packers and Sorters.

It is widely believed that the kind of education one receives and the level of occupation achieved are strongly determined by social class. According to this view, the child of upper-class parents is given preferential treatment by society which enables him to achieve a better education and higher occupational level, while working-class children are disadvantaged by their impoverished environment. The connection between intelligence and occupation arises, it is argued, because of the greater opportunities that intelligent parents are able to offer their children. In other words, many people believe that intelligence is a reflection of social class rather than the other way about. There is, in fact, a certain amount of interaction between these two variables, but as we shall see later on, our intelligence "causes" our social class much more powerfully than the social class of our parents "causes" our intelligence. The connections between IQ and occupation shown above are by no means entirely circular since IQ measures in childhood will predict which children in a family will rise and fall in the social scale compared to the position of their parents. IQ is of course not the only factor determining educational and occupational success, but most courses and jobs have a minimum intellectual requirement which must be met before any other attributes begin to count.

How accurate is the IQ?

There are really two questions involved here. The first question is that of *reliability* — what are the chances that one would get the same score if tested again on another occasion? The measurement of IQ is subject to some error; because it is based upon a sample of one's mental abilities, its stability will depend upon the adequacy of that sample. Obviously, the greater the amount of performance that is sampled (i.e. the longer the test) the more reliable will be the IQ score calculated from it. The two tests which were scored in this book individually took only 10 minutes each to do. This is a very short time by most psychometric standards and it follows that these scores are not very reliable. Some readers may have found that their IQs based on these two short tests differed markedly — perhaps by as much as 20 points. This is not surprising when it is realized that passing or failing a single item can make a difference of 10 or more points on the IQ scale. The IQ score based on the total number of problems solved in the two tests combined is considerably more reliable because it is based on a 20-minute sample of problem solving. This time we could say with some confidence that the "true" IQ is unlikely to be more than 10 points removed from the obtained score. Even so it is possible to do better; properly conducted tests given by professional psychologists take more than an hour and give confidence limits of about plus or minus 5 points, i.e. it can be stated with a fair degree of confidence that the true IQ will be within 5 points of the figure given. For all practical purposes this is an extremely high degree of reliability. Thus if an individual is thinking of undertaking a university course it matters little whether his IQ is 90 or 95 — he would be well advised to forget it. Similarly, it would make little odds whether his IQ was 130 or 135; any difficulties he encountered would more likely be due to other factors such as personality or motivation, rather than insufficient intelligence.

The second thing that people may be thinking of when they question the "accuracy" of IQ tests is discussed by psychologists under the heading of *validity*. This concerns the problem of whether the tests are really measuring what they are supposed to measure, i.e. are they measuring intelligence, something else, or perhaps nothing at all? This is a much more complex question than the previous one, but it was partly answered by pointing out that IQ tests provide the most satisfactory means of predicting educational and occupational success. This, after all, is the purpose for which they were primarily constructed, and they do it very well indeed. Perhaps even more encouraging is the finding that they are not themselves markedly affected by general educational achievement. Coaching on the actual test items will of course improve one's IQ score, and, as we have argued, practice on similar test items, will also do this to a limited extent, but once experience with the testing materials has been equalized the IQ score will not be altered to any great extent. The evidence to support this statement will be outlined later.

There are, however, a number of assumptions involved in IQ testing, which if violated would be bound to lead to invalid results. For example, verbal tests assume that the testee speaks the language in which the test is written. All tests assume that the subject is motivated to do well; this assumption sometimes breaks down, e.g. when an individual is taking the test as part of a job selection programme in which he knows that people with "too much" intelligence are rejected as unlikely to stick at the job. There is also a possibility that exceptionally high motivation to do well can give rise to anxiety which has a debilitating effect on test performance.

Overall, we can say that IQ testing is fairly accurate in the sense of showing adequate reliability and validity when well-designed tests are used by properly qualified psychologists under suitable conditions of testing. Such ideal conditions are not fully met in the self-scoring IQ measure available in this book; it should be regarded as an estimate requiring verification rather than a definitive measure in the individual case. Unless this attitude is adopted the book in your hands is potentially dangerous. You have been warned!

Are differences in IQ caused by nature or nurture?

The major part of variation in intelligence (about 80%) is due to heredity; the environment plays a definite but relatively small part. How do we know? There are several different lines of evidence and they yield results which agree remarkably well. The best known proofs are those that make use of twins. Identical twins result from a single egg which has split after fertilization, and they therefore share a common heredity. The effect of the environment on intelligence can be gauged by comparing the IQs of such twins who have been brought up separately from each other. On average their IQs have been found to differ by 6.6 points, which is only about 2 points greater than the difference to be expected when the same person is tested on two different occasions. In other words, differences in upbringing and other environmental factors add only about 2 points on average to the IQ difference between identical twins. What is more, it doesn't seem to matter at what age the separation took place; one important study found that identical twins were actually *more* alike when they had been separated very early (after two months) than when they had been separated later (around two years).

Another important comparison is that between identical twins and fraternal (two-egg) twins. The latter, like ordinary brothers and sisters, share only 50% of heredity compared to the 100% for identical twins, so if IQ is strongly influenced by heredity we would expect the correlation between them to be considerably lower. This has been found to be the case; on average identical twins correlate .86, fraternal twins .55. This is a substantial difference and it indicates that the IQ is strongly influenced by heredity. It is also possible using a genetic model to predict the extent of other family similarities. Thus if IQ were purely hereditary uncles and aunts would correlate .32 with nephews and nieces, and this compares well with the observed value of .34. Second cousins have rather less common heredity, and we would expect a correlation of .14; the actual correlation of .16 again ties in very well. Again, if genetic factors are important, inbreeding should produce a lowering of IQ in the offspring, a tendency which has been observed in studies of cousin marriages.

One of the most striking proofs of the inheritance of IQ, which has already been hinted at, is the phenomenon of *regression towards the mean*. Children of high IQ parents show a lower intelligence than their parents, while fathers who are unskilled workers produce children brighter than themselves. This regression is observed in all genetically mediated variables (e.g. height) and it is difficult to see how it could be explained in environmentalist terms. If environmental influences were critical we would expect class-based advantage and disadvantage to be cumulative; instead the very reverse is observed (Fig. 2).

Other lines of evidence focus on the control and manipulation of environmental conditions. For example, orphanage conditions expose children to a standard environment, or at least as standard as we could ever wish to see. They have the same teachers, food, buildings, companions, games, excursions and books. Now if high and low IQs stem from good and bad environmental influences respectively, removing the extremes of environment in this way should produce fairly uniform IQs. In fact only a very minor reduction in the amount of variation is observed (less than 10%), which again demonstrates that hereditary factors must predominate. Finally, there is the interesting discovery that foster children correlate in IQ with their biological mothers to about the same extent as children brought up by their own mothers, while correlations with their foster mothers are low or even non-existent. Further, the particular characteristics of the foster home make very little difference; factors such as socio-economic status, number of books, amount of time devoted to the child, and pressure for education, which are often said to be important, make only marginal contributions to the variance in IQs.

All of this evidence adds up to a fairly firm estimate of 80% heritability for the IQ. Environmental effects have also been confirmed but their contribution amounts to no more than about 20% of variation. It is not possible to be too precise with these percentages because they depend to some extent on the kinds of hereditary and environmental extremes that are permitted in the calculation. There are certain kinds of mental deficiency which have a very simple genetic basis and which yield IQs so low that they fall outside of the normal distribution; if these were included in the formulae, the proportion of variation due to inheritance would come out higher still. On the other hand, there are various extreme kinds of environmental intervention such as a bash over the head with a sledge hammer or solitary confinement for the first 15 years of life which, if included in the formulae, would certainly inflate the environmental influence. The figure of 80% heritability is based upon a comparison of the effects of the normal ranges of both genes and environment. Similar figures have been obtained in all other European countries in which the relevant research has been conducted.

Obviously, to the extent that the IQ is genetically determined, it is not possible to alter it by special education or any other form of environmental improvement. Also, as we have said there are definite limits on the extent to which practice on IQ tests will result in improvement in the score obtained on a subsequent test. An effect of this kind can be observed, and hopefully has been observed by the reader in comparing his score on the two short tests in this book, but it is observed only in people who begin as fairly unfamiliar with the kinds of items that appear in IQ tests, and even then it will only amount to a few IQ points (perhaps something of the order of about 8 points).

Are there any other ways to improve IQ?

Nothing that is very firmly established, but there are some interesting new developments in the way of physical treatments. Some claims were recently made that abdominal decompression of expectant mothers during late pregnancy and childbirth resulted in an improvement of about 30% in the mental age of their

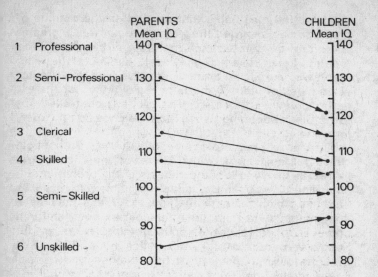

		PARENTS Mean IQ		CHILDREN Mean IQ
1	Professional	140		140
2	Semi–Professional	130		130
		120		120
3	Clerical	115		
4	Skilled	110		110
5	Semi–Skilled	100		100
		90		90
6	Unskilled	80		80

children (the idea being that suction on the outside of the abdomen enlarged the womb and allowed a greater amount of oxygen to reach the brain of the developing foetus). Later research, however, suggests that this result was merely an artifact resulting from the greater willingness of high IQ mothers to volunteer for the experiment. When this effect was properly controlled for, the babies of decompressed mothers showed no superiority in IQ.

More promising are the studies using a chemical called glutamic acid, which (perhaps significantly) is intimately involved in the synthesis of the protein molecule. There has been a steady accumulation of research findings which indicate that doses of this acid have some capacity to raise the intelligence of dull children and mental defectives. It does nothing, however, for people of average or high intelligence. For a while it was thought that the effect might be explained as a correction of dietary deficiency in the less fortunate children with low IQs, and therefore usually low social class, but it now seems to be something more than that. Further research is needed to establish the optimum dosage and the precise mechanism by which this drug operates on the brain to increase intelligence, but exciting developments in this area may be ahead of us.

Are there any racial and national differences in IQ?

Yes there are, although "race" in the sense of skin colour is not the critical factor; "group" or "regional" differences seem more important. Black Americans score on average 15 points lower than white and Oriental Americans. Mexican Americans and American Indians produce scores that are in between these other groups. Considerable differences also appear among various European groups; Irish IQs, for example, average 15 points lower than those of the English.

The origins of these differences remain somewhat obscure, but the weight of evidence points towards a genetic basis for at least some part of them. It is sometimes stated that IQ tests are constructed by middle-class, educated, white city-dwellers for the benefit of themselves and their children. Such a notion is readily demonstrated to be wrong; for example, Canadian Eskimos do not perform badly compared to white Canadians on standard IQ tests, in fact they actually do slightly better. Oriental Americans are certainly not disadvantaged by their minority status; again, if there is any difference at all, they do slightly better than white Americans. Furthermore, attempts to construct "culture fair" tests have consistently failed to reduce the disadvantage of the lower scoring groups. A more probable explanation is that selective migration patterns may have beneficial or deleterious effects on the donor and recipient groups and areas with respect to IQ, by altering the constitution of the gene pool. Thus, in the same way that social mobility has been shown to maintain class differences in IQ, geographical mobility may feed ethnic and national differences. Effects of this kind almost certainly do occur but it is not clear to what extent they would account for the cross-national differences that may be currently observed. There are many other interesting suggestions, such as the idea that black Americans may have reduced IQs because of the infiltration of "poor white blood", or that in Ireland high IQ genes have been peeled off by the infertile priesthood, but there is no real evidence by which to evaluate these hypotheses.

Incidentally, it needs to be stressed that the data concerning racial and national differences in IQ should give scant comfort to racist politicians or others who favour discrimination on grounds of ethnic background. The overlap in intelligence between various groups, even those whose averages are most widely separated, is so enormous that there is no practical justification for discriminating on the basis of race (even if this were morally defensible). There are a great many black people in

America who are more intelligent than the average white, just as there are a great many white people duller than the average black. Race does predict IQ to some extent, but certainly not well enough for it to be a useful basis of discrimination in education or employment. So far from supporting a racist position, the facts are clearly contrary to it.

Are men brighter than women?

No; on overall IQ scores they come out pretty well the same. However, there are two interesting differences between men and women in mental ability. Firstly, men show a greater amount of dispersion; i.e. there are more very bright men and more very dull ones. The reason for this is not well understood. It has been suggested that the greater representation of men in the very high and very low IQ groups might explain why males are over-represented in institutions for the mentally subnormal on the one hand, and produce more works of creative genius on the other. This idea is appealing but there are reasons for mistrusting it. Men are more highly driven both by their biological constitution and the demands that society places upon them; it is conceivable if not likely that these pressures would account for their high productivity and their high drop-out rate.

The second difference between men and women in intelligence relates to the particular abilities in which they each excel. In general, women are superior in language skills such as verbal fluency and vocabulary, in rote memory and manual dexterity; men are superior in visuo-spatial problems, mathematics and reasoning. The evidence is strong that these differences are biologically based rather than culturally determined, which means that they are probably mediated by the effects of sex hormones on the developing structure of the brain. Evidence for the biological origin of these sex differences comes from studies of animals (parallel differences have been observed between male and female rats and other mammals) and developmental studies (differences between boys and girls appear within a few months of birth that seem basic to the differences in adulthood, e.g. girls show greater interest in sound patterns, boys in visual stimuli). Another interesting lead concerning the biological basis of these differences is that linguistic skills are handled primarily by the left hemisphere of the brain while visuo-spatial skills are dealt with more by the right hemisphere. This ties in well with the observation that neuro-anatomical development (e.g. myelination and growth of dendrites) is more advanced in the left hemisphere of young girls and the right hemisphere of boys.

It seems likely that this specialization of abilities in men and women has an evolutionary origin. For example, in mammals generally, the males tend to roam around for purposes of hunting, aggression and defence; females stay at home tending the offspring and so do not require the same visuo-spatial ability. These differences probably also help to explain the different occupations into which males and females drift. Thus men are predominant in occupations requiring mathematical, mechanical, and spatial skills, e.g. engineers and airline pilots (apart from jobs requiring sheer physical strength), while women predominate in secretarial and assembly jobs, where their superior linguistic and manual skills would seem appropriate. This occupational specialization is of course reinforced by social pressures, and sometimes even laws, but it should not be forgotten that there are biological differences between the sexes that are meaningfully connected with the differing social functions of men and women.

Do IQ tests measure creativity and genius?

Not by themselves. Creativity and genius apparently require something in addition to intelligence — probably certain personality characteristics. Perhaps most important are qualities such as drive, assertiveness, arrogance and persistence; these are more characteristic of men than women, which might explain why men throughout history have produced a great deal more creative work. In recent years it has become fashionable to think that the social disadvantages of women are sufficient to account for their relative lack of creative genius, but this notion simply does not accord with the facts. If male predominance was restricted to science and exploration it might be possible to maintain this position, but men have excelled in the arts as well, including even the traditional feminine pursuits like dress designing. No major musical work has ever been composed by a woman despite considerable encouragement in the form of music lessons for young girls, etc. It is also significant that the one field in which women have been able to compete to some extent with men, that of writing novels (witness Jane Austen, the Brontë sisters, George Eliot, Katherine Mansfield, Virginia Woolf) is one that utilizes their superior verbal ability. The best evidence we have suggests that male creativity stems neither from intellectual differences nor social role pressures of arbitrary origin, but from personality differences that are mediated by hormones.

Prediction of creativity and genius, then, requires more than a measure of intelligence. There is no doubt that a high IQ is a strong contributory factor to such productivity but it is not by itself sufficient. The tendency for some writers to arbitrarily equate IQs of over a certain point (say 135) with the term "genius" is misleading and should be discouraged. Genius depends upon other qualities such as drive and perseverance as well. It is sometimes facilitated by thinking of an unusual or nonconformist kind, or by unusual combinations of interests and abilities (e.g. music, mythology and perhaps also sadism in the case of Richard Wagner), but contrary to many prophets of the counter culture, full-blown schizophrenic psychosis is definitely not conducive to creative output of lasting value. There is a slight conceptual problem here, though, in that works of genius are socially defined and there may be disagreement concerning which achievements are worthy of discussion in these terms. However, we can be fairly certain that Galileo, Newton and Einstein were not mad, nor were Da Vinci, Shakespeare and Beethoven.

A number of attempts have been made to design tests specifically to measure creativity rather than ordinary intelligence. Often they make use of open-ended questions such as, "Write down as many uses as you can think of for a brick". The kind of thinking measured by questions such as these is called *divergent*, in contrast to the *convergent* kind of thinking tapped by regular IQ tests in which the problems have only one correct answer. Unfortunately these tests seem to fail in their stated purpose on two counts. Firstly, they correlate quite highly with ordinary convergent tests to such an extent that there is doubt as to whether they measure anything very much different. Secondly, they fail to distinguish truly creative individuals (people who have actually demonstrated their creative ability by what they have produced) from those who are not.

The standard IQ tests are primarily designed to measure important differences around the middle of the population. We know little about the differences between people who score say 140 and 150 because there are so few of them in the population that comparative studies cannot easily be done. In any case most of the tests have a definite ceiling in the sense that a number of individuals get all or nearly all of the problems correct and cannot therefore be distinguished from one another. People of acknowledged genius might be distinguished by exceptionally high IQs on the average but the tests that we commonly use are not geared to making fine distinctions at the extreme ends of the distribution. And since the so-called tests of creativity don't seem to do any better, we will have to wait to see if the future produces anything new as regards assessment of the intellectual components of genius.

Do IQ tests diagnose mental subnormality?

This is what they were initially devised for, and they do it quite successfully. In fact they reveal the existence of two kinds of mental subnormality. There are people with IQs between about 50 and 70 who apparently represent the bottom end of the normal distribution of IQs; they tend to come from homes where the parents are of low IQ and there are likely to be other mental defectives in the family. Then there is another group sometimes called "imbeciles", who are of even lower IQ but who may come from any sort of home and whose parents show an IQ range which does not differ markedly from the normal population. The latter groups are apparently suffering from a single gene disorder which, because it is recessive, has been passed on by parents who did not themselves manifest defectiveness. The presence of this group in the population gives rise to a small bump on the bottom end of the normal IQ distribution, causing its bell shape to be slightly less perfect than that depicted earlier.

There is no equivalent abnormality detectable by standard IQ tests that provides a bump at the top half of the distribution, but there has been some interesting speculation that autistic and idiot-savant children represent variants of extremely high intelligence. These are children who show intellectual impairment in many areas, but outstanding talent in certain highly specialized areas such as music and mathematics. There is some evidence that such children are more likely to come from high IQ parents than are normal children.

At what age is peak intelligence reached?

This is a very complex question. If we examine performance on IQ tests without any allowance for age being made, we find that intelligence increases sharply through childhood, reaches a plateau in the late teens, and then stays fairly steady until middle age when it begins to tail off again. But this graph is really the resultant of two others which could be described as *knowledge* and *brain power* — roughly equivalent in cybernetic terms to memory store and information processing capacity. (See Fig. 3.)

There is a sense in which our brain power declines from the moment of birth. Our flexibility and eagerness to learn are probably then at a maximum, and we never have more nerve cells in our brain than at that time (increases in the size of our brain as we grow up are due to enlargement of connective and insulating tissues, not nerve cells themselves). As we move into our adult years our brain cells begin to die at a faster rate, and probably as a result we become progressively fixed in our modes of thinking. However, our "brain power" is also determined by maturational processes, which cause it, on balance, to increase up to the age of about 16. The other major factor involved in intelligence is the accumulation of knowledge acquired as a result of experience. This increases our effectiveness in dealing with the environment right through into our middle age, when it is likely to be called "wisdom". Our peak of measured ability is a result of the interplay between these two curves. At birth we are not very useful to ourselves or society because our knowledge and maturity are at minimum. After the age of 50 or so our accomplishments tail off because our brain power is declining at such a rate that our continuing experience can no longer compensate; in fact, as our brain power drops we even lose the capacity to benefit from experience. Somewhere in the middle of our life span, between the ages of about 25 and 40, we are at a peak as far as intellectual output is concerned.

The precise age of maximum intelligence depends on the relative importance of the two major components to the skills being used in assessing it. Thus tasks which depend on originality rather than experience (e.g. mathematics and inventing) show an earlier peak than skills which require greater wisdom (e.g. writing a novel or history book). A survey by H. C. Lehman in 1953 showed that "outstanding accomplishments" of great men and women were achieved at different ages depending on the field of endeavour. Poets tended to produce their greatest works between 25 and 29, scientists between 30 and 34, medical men and philosophers between 35 and 39. Fiction writers and painters showed a greater variability as regards their peak years, which were given as ranging from 30 to 45. It should not be forgotten that great works are often produced by people much older than this; Verdi, for example, was in his late seventies when he wrote "Otello" and "Falstaff", which are admired by musicians as two of the greatest operas ever written. On the other hand, we should also appreciate that younger men between about 16 and 25 probably have greater power and flexibility in their thinking than men in the years of "peak achievement". Often a creative thinker, be he artist or scientist, has his best ideas when very young but is well into his thirties or forties by the time they have been fully developed and presented to the world.

Does intelligence really matter?

Many people object that psychologists put too much emphasis on intelligence because it is not a measure of a man's worth. Of course there are a great many other human qualities that are cited as praiseworthy, e.g. compassion, altruism, bravery, reliability, and honesty; one can be highly intelligent without being in the slightest bit distinguished in these other ways. What is more, a high IQ is a personal asset, not necessarily a moral virtue. All it means is that the person is good at learning, thinking abstractly and solving problems; like nuclear power, this capacity can be used for good or ill.

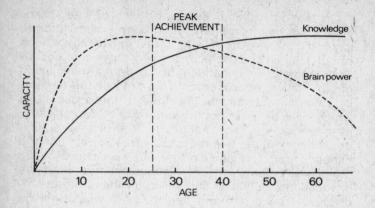

On the other hand, the importance of intelligence should not be underestimated. It is no exaggeration to say that improvement of living conditions for all sections of our society, and probably the very survival of society as we know it, are dependent on the proper deployment of our intellectual resources. This can be achieved only by ensuring that people are fitted to the occupations which make best use of their various talents, regardless of their age, sex, race, national, social or even educational background. In a reasonably free society this will happen naturally to some extent, but if we can refine the process with the use of intelligence and aptitude tests in vocational guidance and selection then both the individuals concerned and society as a whole will be beneficiaries. As Eysenck has said: "Intelligence is not all there is to man; nevertheless, intelligence is an important and socially extremely useful part of man. Our ability to measure this variable with some degree of precision means that we can control it and use it to the general advantage of society."

NOTES

NOTES

NOTES

NOTES

NOTES

NOTES

NOTES

NOTES

NOTES

NOTES

NOTES

NOTES